ABDO Publishing Company

BUGS!
Ticks

Kristin Petrie

South Huntington Pub. Lib.
145 Pidgeon Hill Rd.
Huntington Sta., N.Y. 11746

visit us at
www.abdopublishing.com

Published by ABDO Publishing Company, 8000 West 78th Street, Edina, Minnesota 55439. Copyright © 2009 by Abdo Consulting Group, Inc. International copyrights reserved in all countries. No part of this book may be reproduced in any form without written permission from the publisher. The Checkerboard Library™ is a trademark and logo of ABDO Publishing Company.

Printed in the United States.

Cover Photo: Corbis
Interior Photos: Alamy pp. 13, 14, 21, 23, 24–25; AP Images p. 29; Corbis pp. 1, 20; Getty Images pp. 15, 19; iStockphoto pp. 4, 5, 19, 26, 28; Mark Plonsky p. 9; Peter Ambruzs/CritterZone.com pp. 7, 16, 22; Peter Arnold p. 27; Photo Researchers p. 11; Scott Bauer/USDA.gov p. 19

Series Coordinator: BreAnn Rumsch
Editors: Megan M. Gunderson, BreAnn Rumsch
Art Direction & Cover Design: Neil Klinepier

Library of Congress Cataloging-in-Publication Data

Petrie, Kristin, 1970-
  Ticks / Kristin Petrie.
    p. cm. -- (Bugs!)
  Includes index.
  ISBN 978-1-60453-072-8
  1. Ticks--Juvenile literature. I. Title.

QL458.15.P37P48 2009
595.4'29--dc22
                                2008005928

Contents

Tricky Ticks 4
What Are They? 6
Body Parts 8
The Inside Story 12
Transformation 14
Hanging Out 20
Fresh Food 22
Beware! 24
Ticks and You 26
Glossary 30
How Do You Say That? 31
Web Sites 31
Index 32

Tricky Ticks

Summertime is perfect for exploring the great outdoors. Camping and hiking in the woods can be fun. So can lying on a sunny patch of grass, rolling down a hill, and sitting by a campfire.

By the end of an active day outside, you're ready to snuggle into your sleeping bag.

But wait! There's a tiny little tickle on your foot. Now it's on your leg. Then it's behind your knee. You jump out of your bag to see what's there. It's a tick!

You jump up and down and try to brush it off. But the tick won't come off. You try to scrape it off with your fingernails. It's still locked on tight.

Being aware of ticks can help prevent tick bites. This means you can still enjoy the outdoor activities you love most!

When a tick decides you will make a juicy meal, you may end up with an uncomfortable bite.

Finally, you manage to get the stubborn bug off your knee. But in that short time, the tiny tick grew. It's pretty obvious what made it swell, too. The tick's red, liquid food was your blood!

Yes, the great outdoors provides a lot of fun, fresh-air activities. Yet woods, fields, and forests are also the land of bugs. And for many humans, the tick is far from a favorite.

What Are They?

Many of us think of ticks as insects, like beetles and ants. In reality, ticks are arachnids from the class Arachnida. Other arachnids include spiders, scorpions, and mites.

Arachnids differ from insects in several ways. They have eight legs instead of six. And, they do not have distinct body **segments**. Arachnids don't have antennae or wings either.

All ticks belong to the order Acarina. **Entomologists** divide this order into two main families. Hard-bodied ticks belong to the family Ixodidae. Soft-bodied ticks belong to the family Argasidae. Altogether, there are about 850 tick species in the world.

Each species of tick has a two-word name called a binomial. A binomial combines the genus with a descriptive name, or epithet. For example, a lone star tick's binomial is *Amblyomma americanum*.

Hard or soft, discovering either kind of tick on yourself is gross! However, keep reading to learn some interesting facts about these creepy, crawly bugs. You'll still want to keep them off your body. But, you may dislike them a little less.

Black-legged ticks are one of the most common hard tick species in the United States. They are also known as deer ticks.

THAT'S CLASSIFIED!

Scientists use a method called scientific classification to sort the world's living organisms into groups. Eight groups make up the basic classification system. In descending order, they are domain, kingdom, phylum, class, order, family, genus, and species.

The phrase "Dear King Philip, come out for goodness' sake!" may help you remember this order. The first letter of each word is a clue for each group.

Domain is the most basic group. Species is the most specific group. Members of a species share common characteristics. Yet, they are different from all other living things in at least one way.

Body Parts

Ticks have a variety of appearances. They range in color from dark brown to reddish brown. Ticks also range in body size. Some are as small as the period at the end of this sentence. Others grow to be more than one inch (3 cm) long!

The tick's body is oval shaped. It consists of a **gnathosoma** and an abdomen. A hard tick also has a scutum. This shieldlike structure covers the top of the tick's abdomen.

Some hard tick species have one to three pairs of simple eyes called ocelli. These eyes help the tick sense light and dark, as well as movement. They are located near the back of the scutum. Other tick species do not have eyes and are blind.

Like all **arthropods**, ticks are covered by a layer of chitin. This hardened substance forms an exoskeleton. A tick's exoskeleton acts like a frame for the rest of its body. It determines the tick's body shape and protects its **organs**.

Despite this stiff outer layer, a tick's abdomen is specially designed to expand. This is vital, because ticks eat until they can hold no more!

Four pairs of jointed legs connect to the abdomen. They allow the tick to scurry around quickly. Each leg ends in a claw. The first set of legs also has Haller's **organs**. They detect carbon dioxide. Animals and people produce this gas when they breathe. Sensing breath and body heat helps lead the tick to possible **hosts**.

The **gnathosoma** features the tick's mouthparts. The largest of these parts are the palpi. Palpi look and work like feelers. They help the tick taste and smell. When a tick feeds, the palpi move out of the way. Their job is to support the tick's other mouthparts.

These mouthparts include the chelicerae and the hypostome. The chelicerae sit between the palpi. They have bladelike points. The tick uses them to cut into its host's skin.

Next, the hypostome penetrates the cut. This mouthpart works like a straw. The tick uses it to drink its liquid meals. The underside of the hypostome is **barbed**. This helps the tick stay attached to its host.

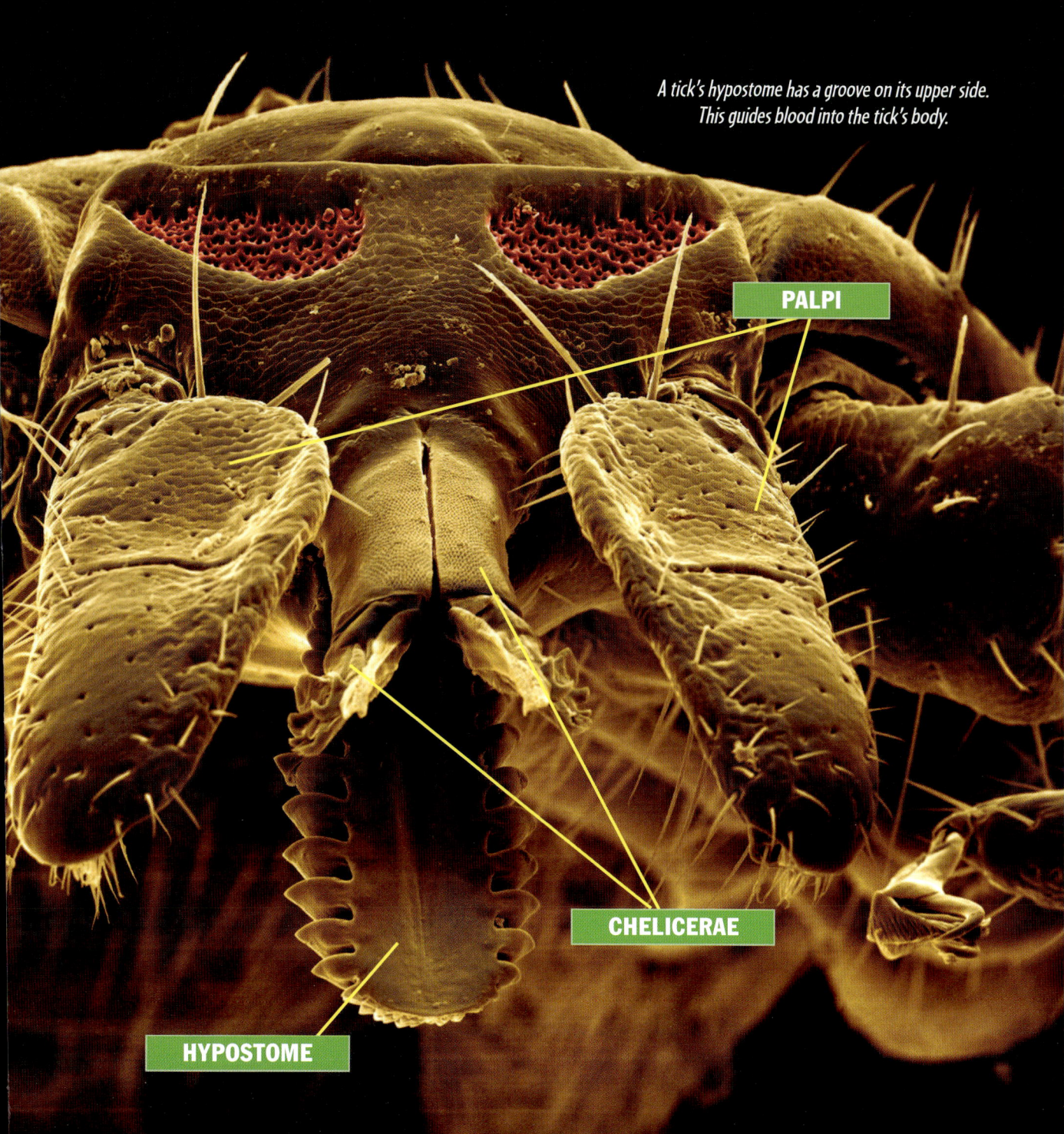

The Inside Story

A tick may be tiny, but many important functions take place inside its body. Several systems and **organs** work together to help the tick survive.

A tick has an open circulatory system. This means blood flows freely within its body. Tick blood is called hemolymph. The tick has a tube-shaped heart. This simple heart pumps hemolymph into different areas of the tick's body.

The tick's respiratory system is made of spiracles and tracheae. Spiracles are holes in the tick's abdomen that let it breathe in oxygen. From the spiracles, air enters tubes called tracheae. They carry the air to the rest of the tick's body.

The tick's nervous system consists of a brain and a **nerve** cord. The nerve cord connects the brain to the abdomen. Smaller nerves extend from the cord throughout the tick's body. Some of these nerves control the tick's legs, muscles, and stomach. Other nerves control the mouthparts.

Soft ticks have a much different appearance than their hard tick cousins. Yet, both tick families rely on the same organs and body systems for survival.

Transformation

The tick's life cycle has four stages. These are egg, larva, nymph, and adult. Passing through these stages is known as complete **metamorphosis**. Yet, the life cycle cannot take place until a male and female tick mate.

After mating, soft ticks and hard ticks behave differently. A female soft tick lays several hundred eggs onto her **host** animal. She will continue to feed and lay eggs for the rest of her life. In total, she will lay about 1,000 eggs.

A male hard tick may remain on his host after mating. Unlike a female hard tick, the male may mate several times before completing his life cycle.

A female hard tick drops off her host and lays eggs only once. However, she may lay up to 6,000 eggs! A hard tick mother has a

BUG BYTES
Some female hard ticks need up to 15 days to lay their entire batch of eggs!

special way of making sure her eggs are safe. As she lays her eggs, she passes them over her mouthparts. This coats the eggs with a substance that protects them from drying out.

After laying her eggs, the female hard tick will die. To protect her eggs, she deposits them in a safe place. This might be onto soil, plants, or fallen leaves.

The more blood a female tick eats, the more eggs she will be able to produce.

Since ticks cannot jump or fly, they must come in direct contact with hosts. Questing helps ticks hitch a ride on new hosts.

Ticks remain in their eggs for several weeks. This exact length of time depends on the species. It also depends on the season the eggs are laid in and the temperature of their surroundings.

Most tick eggs hatch in the spring. The eggs break to reveal tiny baby ticks. These larvae look like adult ticks, with one difference. They have only six legs.

A soft tick larva remains near a **host**'s nest. Whenever the host returns to its nest, the larva has an easy food source. Hard tick larvae are not so lucky. They must search for their first meal.

This search for food is called questing. The hard tick larva begins by climbing to the edge of a leaf or a blade of grass. Next, the larva holds its legs out. It hopes to snag a host walking by.

Once a host has been found, the larva feeds until it nearly bursts. After its blood meal, the larva falls off its host. Next, its full stomach helps its tight skin split and fall off. Underneath, a shiny new exoskeleton and an extra set of legs are revealed. This process is called molting.

After molting, the larva enters the nymphal stage. A nymph is larger than a larva and has all eight legs. Like the larva, the nymph's job is to find a new **host** and eat.

After eating, the nymph falls off its host and molts again. Hard ticks enter the adult stage after this molt. However, soft tick nymphs feed and molt many times before becoming adults.

Can you guess what the adult tick does? It searches for food! Some adult ticks get lucky and nab a host right away. Species in cold climates may wait up to three years before finding a host. These ticks **hibernate** until a new host becomes available.

When they have gorged on their blood meals, adult ticks find a mate. A female hard tick's life cycle ends after mating and laying eggs a single time. Soft tick species feed and reproduce many times before their life cycle ends.

The life span of many hard tick species is less than one year. Yet this time period may lengthen, depending on the tick's climate. Soft ticks can live much longer than hard ticks. In fact, some species have been known to live as long as ten years!

BUG BYTES

Black-legged ticks take two years to complete their life cycle.

LIFE CYCLE OF A TICK

EGG

ADULT

LARVA

NYMPH

Hanging Out

Amblyomma hebraeum *males have beautiful markings on their abdomens. This tick species was brought into the United States from Africa.*

You can probably name several likely places to find ticks. These include the wooded areas near your tent and that grassy hill you like to roll down. But did you know that ticks also survive in the desert? Ticks can be found in the coldest places on Earth as well.

This means that ticks live everywhere from Antarctica to the Arctic. In the United States, ticks are found in every state. How can this be? Ticks can live anywhere they can find a **host**!

Some ticks are named for their host. These special names include chicken, cattle, dog, sheep, and wood ticks. However, most

BUG BYTES

Soft ticks live in caves, stables, and nests. They come out of their hiding places at night to attack their sleeping hosts.

ticks are not picky. They will make themselves at home on many types of **hosts**. Common favorites include dogs and deer. Other popular hosts are reptiles and birds. Last but not least, ticks love to feed on humans.

Once a tick finds a host, it burrows through hair and fur until it reaches skin. Then, the tick uses its mouthparts to pierce the host's skin and clamp on. In addition, hard ticks **secrete** a sticky substance into the wound. This allows them to hold on even tighter!

A female lone star tick is easily recognized by the white spot on her back. These ticks are abundant in the southern United States. They range from Texas to Florida.

Fresh Food

Here's the worst part about these bugs. A tick's diet consists of a single food, blood! Sometimes it is your blood. This habit of feeding on a **host** makes a tick an **ectoparasite**.

Many tick species are not picky about their food sources. In its lifetime, a hard tick may feed on many different creatures. So, these ticks are often identified by the number of hosts they have.

For example, a one-host tick spends its life cycle on a single host. A two-host tick feeds off one animal

A male hard tick's scutum covers most of its back. This limits how much it can expand. Therefore, males eat less blood than females do.

BUG BYTES

Soft ticks are able to complete a meal in as little as two minutes. On the other hand, hard ticks may feed for up to 72 hours.

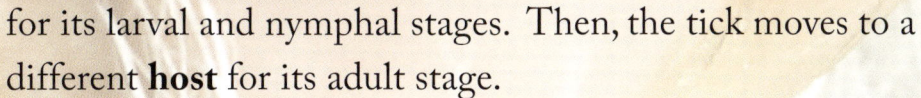

for its larval and nymphal stages. Then, the tick moves to a different **host** for its adult stage.

Last are the three-host ticks. Can you guess what these ticks do? They feast on one host for their larval stage. They choose a second host for the nymphal stage and a third for the adult stage. This type of hard tick is most common.

Hard ticks can grow more than ten times their normal weight in one feeding.

Beware!

Most creatures just have to live with these annoying bugs. For example, a cow can't reach around and pick off a tick. Few animals have this ability. Humans are the lucky ones. We have the fingers and the tools to remove ticks.

Ticks do have natural enemies. Reptiles, insects, and even other arachnids eat ticks. Small animals such as mice look for blood-filled ticks to fill their stomachs. Birds such as chickens and oxpeckers also eat ticks.

Other natural enemies help control the tick population, too. For example, certain wasp species **inject** their eggs into tick larvae. When the eggs hatch, the newborn wasps eat the ticks!

How do ticks defend themselves? It appears that these bugs have just one defense. They hold on as tight as they can. A hard tick's grip is very strong. The tick's mouthparts may even stay in a **host** as its abdomen is pulled off!

In Africa, deerlike impalas depend on oxpeckers to peck blood-filled ticks from their bodies. These birds also peck ticks off of rhinoceroses, giraffes, buffalo, and cattle.

Ticks and You

American dog ticks are one species that spreads Rocky Mountain spotted fever.

There are many good reasons for humans to avoid ticks. Reason number one is that ticks bite! Most tick bites aren't dangerous. However, they may cause swelling and pain. Several tick species carry dangerous diseases. They spread the diseases when they feed on **hosts**. One of the most common illnesses spread by ticks is Lyme disease. Lyme disease causes sore joints and affects the heart and the nervous system. Another illness spread by ticks is Rocky Mountain spotted fever. This is a very serious disease. If not treated early, it will cause death.

With such serious diseases at hand, it is wise to protect yourself from ticks. How do you do this? Be aware! Before enjoying the

BUG BYTES

Nymphs must feed for more than 24 hours to transmit Lyme disease. Adults take more than 48 hours to pass the disease to their hosts.

great outdoors, think about the places you will be. Will you camp in the woods? Will you walk through grassy fields? These are favorite spots for ticks.

THERE'S A TICK ON ME!

If you find a tick on yourself, let an adult know right away. The tick should be removed as soon as possible. But use caution! Yanking a tick off quickly is not the way to go. This can cause the tick's mouthparts to remain in your skin.

Using substances such as rubbing alcohol is also not effective. This may even cause the tick to spit its stomach contents into the bite.

Instead, have an adult use a tweezers to get ahold of the tick. This instrument should be placed as close to the skin as possible. That way, it is gripping the tick's mouthparts rather than its body. The tick should be pulled gently and slowly away from the skin.

If you develop a ringlike rash or feel unwell, visit your doctor. These are common signs of Lyme disease. Your doctor can give you medicine to treat this illness.

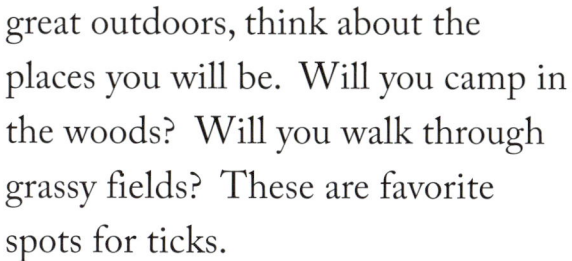

Deer ticks are responsible for the spread of Lyme disease.

Ticks can be very hard to detect, especially in their early stages of life. Dressing appropriately will help you eliminate hiding places for these bloodsuckers.

Your best defense against ticks is to cover up. This means wearing long-sleeved shirts and long pants. Socks and shoes are a must. Tucking your pants into tall boots is a great idea. Pull long hair back, and wear a hat! You'll look cool, and you'll be less likely to serve as a **host** to a tick.

When you're finished with outdoor activities, check your body for ticks. They like to hide in your hair, on your waist, and under

BUG BYTES

The tick population is at its height during June and July. However, tick bites are common anytime between April and October.

your arms. If a tick has succeeded in sucking your blood, stay calm. Diseases are not passed immediately from tick to **host**.

Ask an adult to remove the tick. Also, save its body. If you become sick, the tick may need to be identified. However, the chances of it being a disease-spreading species are low.

Don't be afraid of ticks. You can still get outside and explore the great outdoors!

You now know a little more about ticks. You may still dislike having to share the outdoors with these bugs. However, you may be less grossed out the next time you see one. You will also know how to stay safe while enjoying time outside.

Glossary

arthropod - any of a phylum of invertebrate animals that includes insects, arachnids, and crustaceans. An arthropod has a segmented body, jointed limbs, and an exoskeleton.
barbed - having barbs. Barbs are sharp projections that extend backward and prevent easy extraction. A fishhook is a common example of an object with a barb.
ectoparasite - a parasite that lives outside its host's body. A parasite is an organism that lives off of another organism of a different species.
entomologist - a scientist who studies insects.
gnathosoma - a primary region of an arachnid's body, which consists of the mouthparts.
hibernate - to spend a period of time, such as the winter, in an inactive state.
host - a living animal or plant on or in which a parasite lives.
inject - to forcefully introduce a substance into something.
metamorphosis - the process of change in the form and habits of some animals during development from an immature stage to an adult stage.
nerve - one of the stringy bands of nervous tissue that carries signals from the brain to other organs.
organ - a part of an animal or a plant that is composed of several kinds of tissues and that performs a specific function. The heart, liver, gallbladder, and intestines are organs of an animal.
secrete - to form and give off.
segment - any of the parts into which a thing is divided or naturally separates.

How Do You Say That?

Acarina - a-kuh-REEN-uh
antennae - an-TEH-nee
Arachnida - uh-RAK-nuhd-uh
Argasidae - ahr-GAS-uh-dee
chelicerae - kih-LIH-suh-ree
chitin - KEYE-tuhn
entomologist - ehn-tuh-MAH-luh-jihst
gnathosoma - nay-thoh-SOH-muh
hemolymph - HEE-muh-lihmf
hypostome - HEYE-puh-stohm
Ixodidae - ihk-SAHD-uh-dee
larvae - LAHR-vee
metamorphosis - meh-tuh-MAWR-fuh-suhs
nymph - NIHMF
ocelli - oh-SEH-leye
scutum - SKOO-tuhm
tracheae - TRAY-kee-ee

Web Sites

To learn more about ticks, visit ABDO Publishing Company on the World Wide Web at **www.abdopublishing.com**. Web sites about ticks are featured on our Book Links page. These links are routinely monitored and updated to provide the most current information available.

Index

A
abdomen 8, 10, 12, 24
Acarina (order) 6
Arachnida (class) 6, 24
Argasidae (family) 6

B
binomial 6

C
cattle tick 20
chicken tick 20
circulatory system 12
classification 6
color 8

D
defense 15, 24
diet 5, 10, 14, 17, 18, 21, 22, 23, 24, 26, 29
disease 26, 29
dog tick 20

E
ectoparasite 22
enemies 24
entomologist 6
exoskeleton 8, 10, 17
eyes 8

G
gnathosoma 8, 10

H
Haller's organs 10
hemolymph 12
hibernating 18
homes 5, 20, 21, 27, 29
host 10, 14, 17, 18, 20, 21, 22, 23, 24, 26, 28, 29
human interaction 4, 5, 6, 10, 21, 22, 24, 26, 27, 28, 29

I
Ixodidae (family) 6

L
legs 6, 10, 12, 17, 18
life cycle 14, 15, 17, 18, 22, 23, 24
lone star tick 6

M
molting 17, 18
mouthparts 10, 12, 15, 21, 24

N
nerves 12
nervous system 12

O
organs 8, 12, 17

P
prevention 26, 27, 28, 29

Q
questing 17

R
reproduction 14, 18
respiratory system 12

S
scutum 8
senses 8, 10
shape 8, 12
sheep tick 20
size 5, 8, 12, 17, 18
spiracles 12

T
tracheae 12

W
wood tick 20